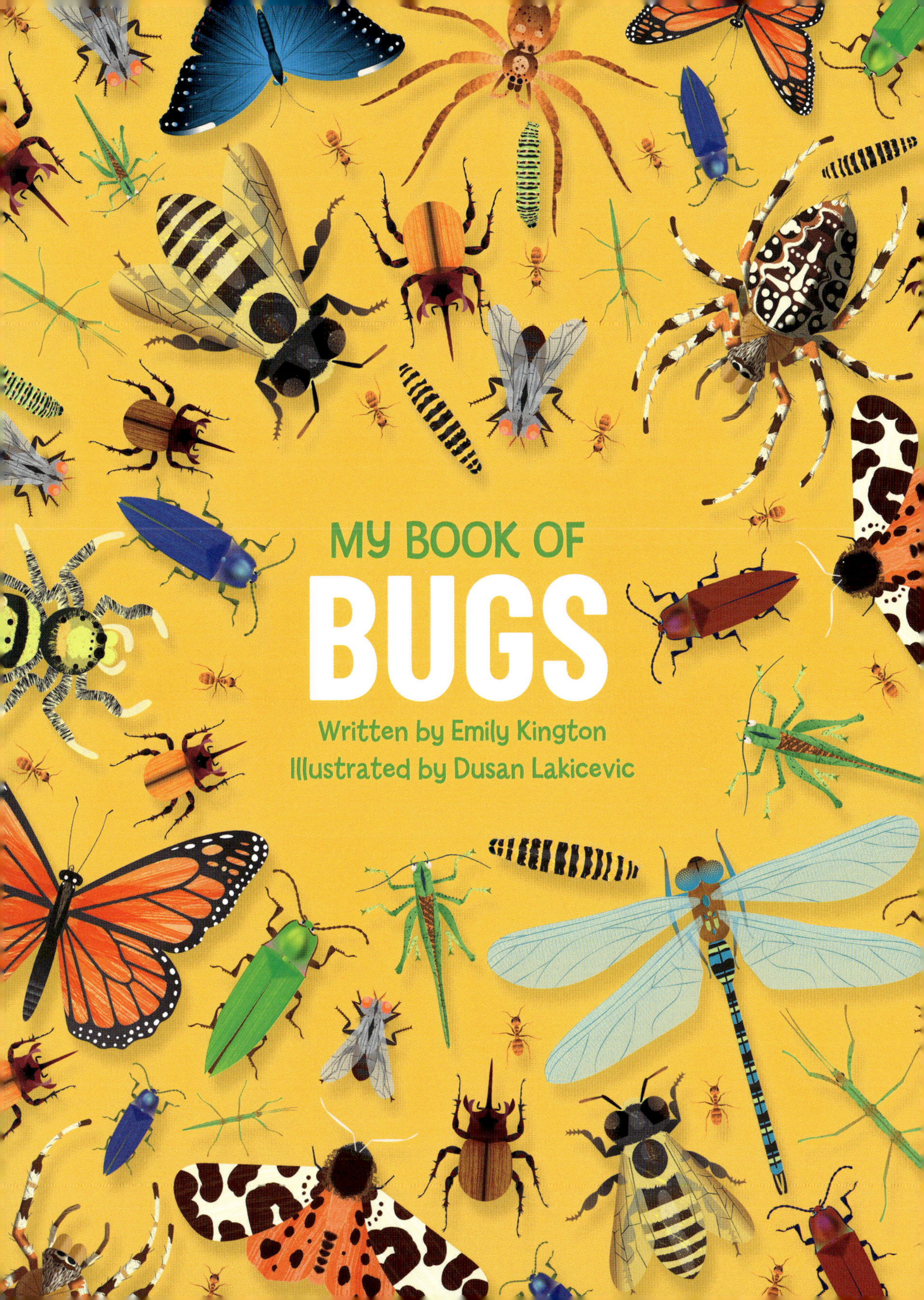

MY BOOK OF BUGS

Written by Emily Kington

Illustrated by Dusan Lakicevic

CONTENTS

HUNGRY TOMATO

First published in 2026 by Hungry Tomato Ltd
F15, Old Bakery Studios, Blewetts Wharf, Malpas Road, Truro, Cornwall,
TR1 1QH, UK.

A CIP catalog record for this book is available from the
British Library.

ISBN 9781835694428

Manufactured in the USA

Discover more at
www.hungrytomato.com

Words in BOLD can be found in the glossary.

WHAT ARE BUGS?

Bugs are all AROUND US!

Our planet is crawling with bugs; wherever you go in the world you will find them!

Why bugs matter!

Bugs keep nature healthy by eating up dead plants and animals. This helps to stop germs from spreading. Their poop even helps plants to grow too!

Bug hunt

You can find them underground, in the air, in the water, and even in your home!

What makes an insect an insect?

All insects have three body parts: a head, thorax, and abdomen. They can also have wings, six legs, and antennae.

Not all bugs are insects, but lots of them are! Turn the page to discover some super busy bugs.

ANT

Ants are EVERYWHERE!

They live in groups, called colonies, and build nests with lots of tunnels. Some nests have more than one million ants living inside them!

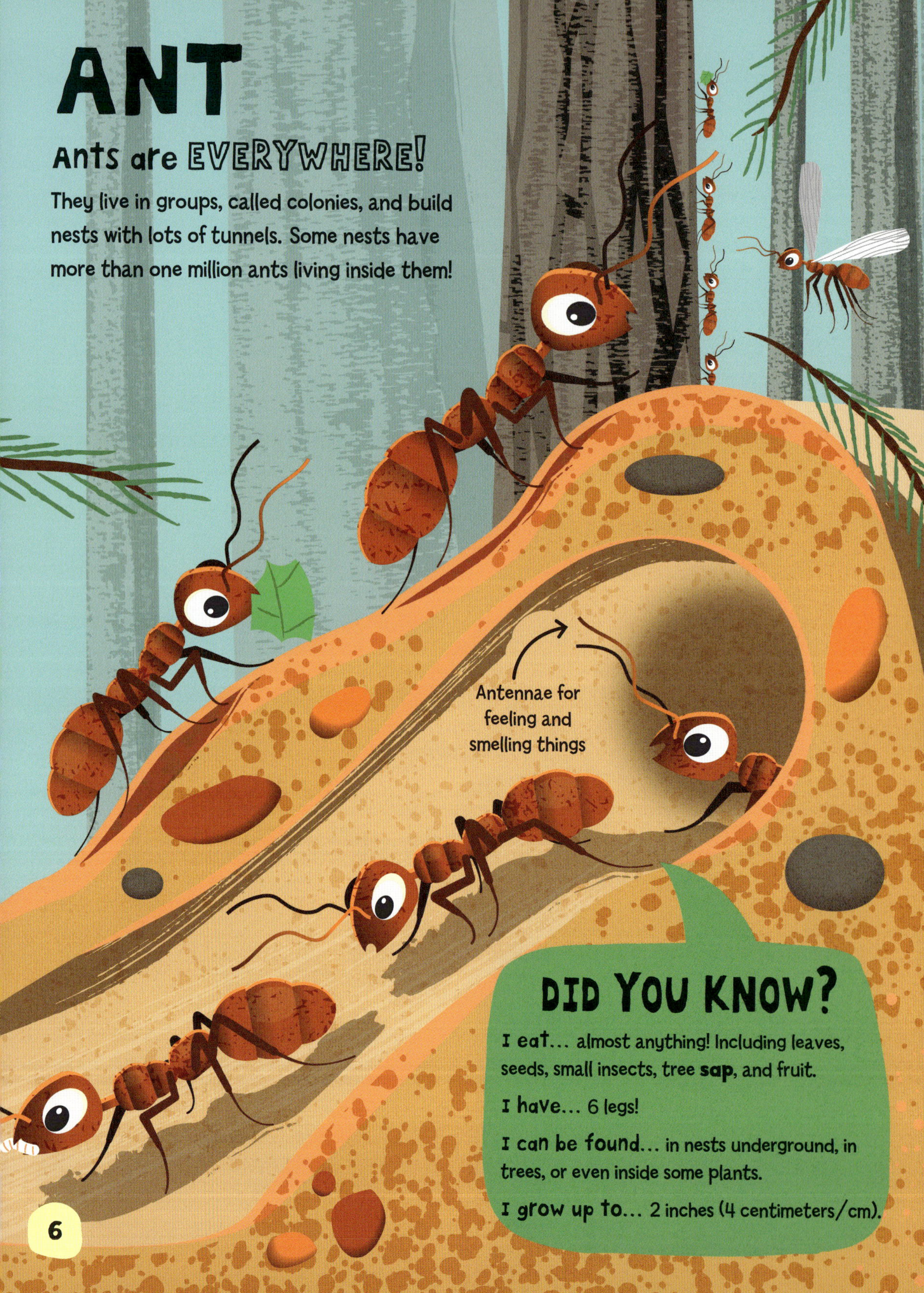

DID YOU KNOW?

I eat... almost anything! Including leaves, seeds, small insects, tree **sap**, and fruit.

I have... 6 legs!

I can be found... in nests underground, in trees, or even inside some plants.

I grow up to... 2 inches (4 centimeters/cm).

Male ants have
wings and are
called drones.
Worker ants build
and look after the
nest, and search
for food.

HONEYBEE

Being a honeybee is a BUSY, BUZZY BUSINESS.

Bees fly from flower to flower collecting sweet **nectar** to make into honey. They spread **pollen** as they go, helping plants to make new seeds.

See-through wings

Pollen sticks to the hair on their legs and body.

Take care - some bees have a stinger!
DID YOU KNOW?
I eat... nectar and pollen from flowers.
I have... 6 legs and 5 eyes!
I can be found... in forests, gardens, or meadows, where flowers grow.
I grow up to... 1 inch (25 millimeters/mm).
The antennae are used to touch, smell, and taste.

EARTHWORM

THESE WIGGLY, WRIGGLY WORMS LIVE UNDERGROUND.

They don't have any legs but are covered in tiny hairs, which help them **burrow** through the soil. Worms help to keep soil healthy, which is good for plants and other animals.

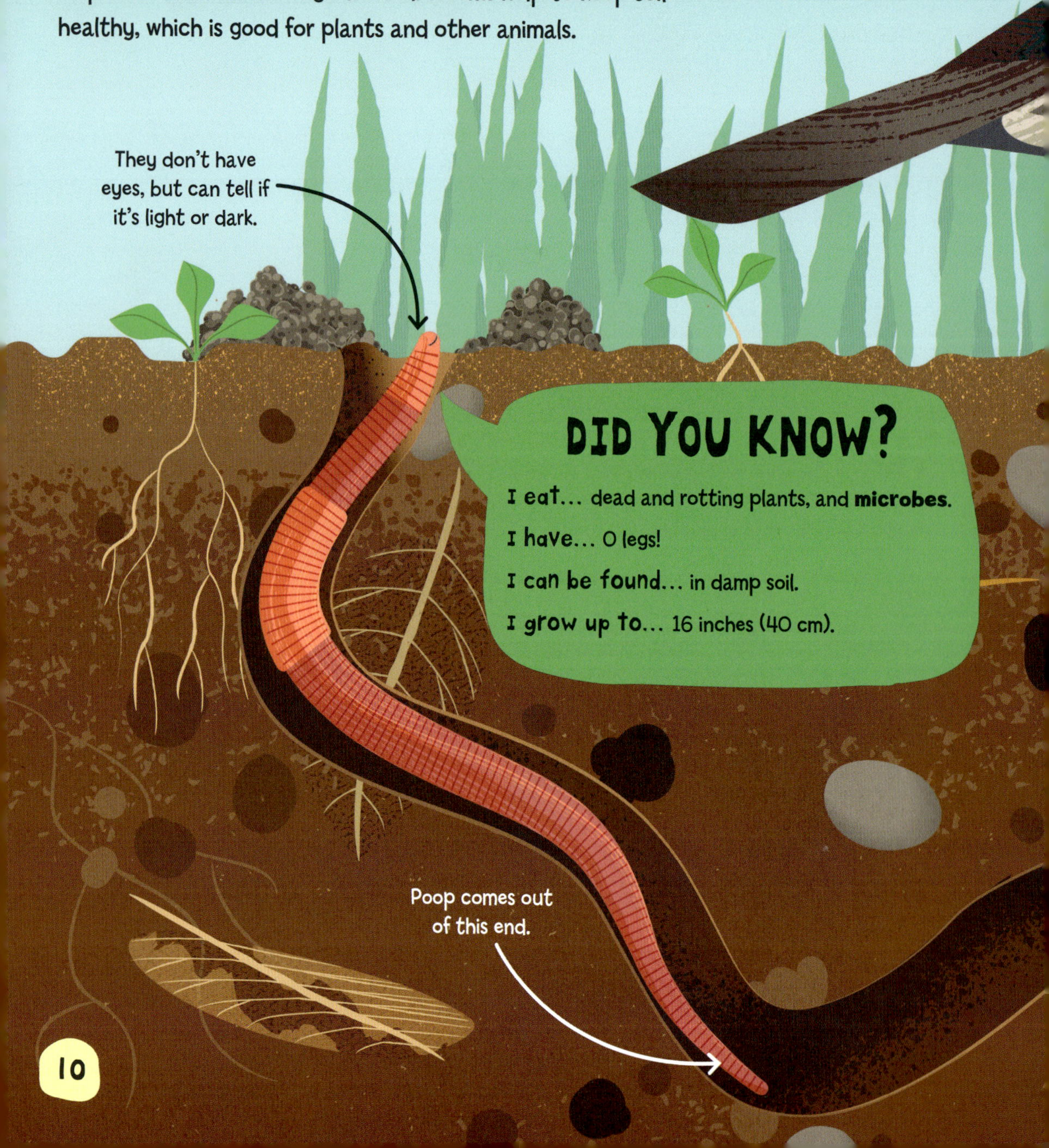

They don't have eyes, but can tell if it's light or dark.

DID YOU KNOW?

I eat… dead and rotting plants, and **microbes**.

I have… 0 legs!

I can be found… in damp soil.

I grow up to… 16 inches (40 cm).

Poop comes out of this end.

Worms may not look very tasty, but birds love them!
Long tube-shaped body, made of lots of **segments**
Mouth

SNAIL

Snails are SOFT, SLIMY creatures with a hard shell on their back.

Snails are born with their shells and can curl up inside them to hide from danger. They normally live for 3 to 7 years.

DID YOU KNOW?
I eat... plants and **fungi**. Sometimes I even eat worms, slugs, and other snails!
I have... 0 legs!
I can be found... in dark, damp places. Some of us even live in water.
I grow up to... 15 inches (38cm).
Inside its mouth are thousands of teeth.
Snails can be different sizes.

BEETLES

These bright bugs help to keep soil HEALTHY!

They can look very different and come in lots of shapes and sizes. They have hard wing cases to protect their fragile wings.

Some beetles are
bright and shiny, like
beautiful gems.
DID YOU KNOW?
I eat... almost anything! Some of us eat plants, other insects, dead animals, or even poop!
I have... 6 legs!
I can be found... almost everywhere around the world.
I grow up to... 8 inches (19 cm).

CATERPILLAR

These GREEDY GRUBS spend almost all their time eating!

They may not look like it, but they are actually baby butterflies or moths. Once they are fully grown, they start to change into the completely different shape of a butterfly or moth ...wow! Turn the page to see what they turn into!

Caterpillars have 6 legs, but they also have extra stumpy **prolegs** to help them move and grip onto things.
DID YOU KNOW?
I eat... plants, especially leaves, flowers, and fruit.
I have... 6 legs!
I can be found... almost anywhere!
I grow up to... 5 inches (13 cm).
Caterpillars make a **chrysalis** like this to live in while they change shape!

BUTTERFLY

What bright and beautiful WINGS!

Can you believe this butterfly was once a caterpillar? Their wings can be lots of different patterns and shapes. Butterflies love to fly around in the sunshine, which helps to keep them warm.

DID YOU KNOW?
I eat... sweet liquids, including nectar, fruit juice, and tree sap.
I have... 6 legs!
I can be found... almost anywhere!
I grow up to... 11 inches (28 cm).
Butterflies use their feet to taste!
Long, curled mouthpart for reaching nectar
Thin antennae help them smell and balance.

MORE GREAT BUGS

There are so many fascinating bugs around the world to learn about. How many of these have you spotted in the wild before?

SLUG

Greedy slugs eat just about anything! Most gardeners think they are real **pests** because they can cause a lot of damage to their plants. Slugs have soft, slimy bodies with no bones and no legs! They are like snails without a shell.

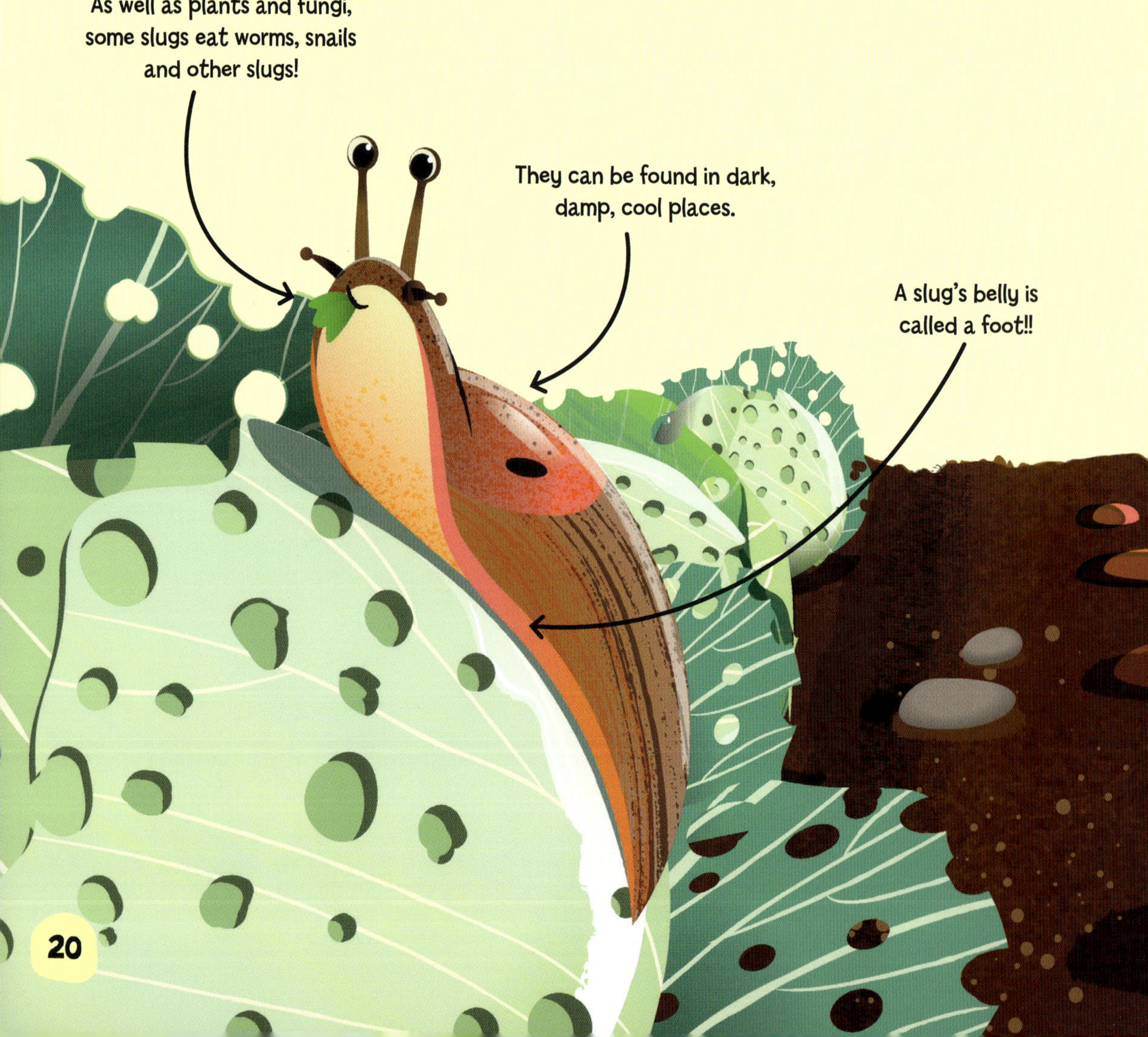

FIREFLY

These beautiful glow-in-the-dark bugs are not flies at all - they're beetles! They make their own light using special organs inside their bellies in order to send messages to each other.

SPIDER

Spiders are known for making webs, which you might have even seen in corners of your home! Different types of spiders are found all over the world, from dry deserts to your bathtub!

WHAT'S THAT BUG?

With millions of different types of bug out there, it can be difficult to tell them apart! Here's a chart to help you identify some of the different bugs, including some that aren't in this book!

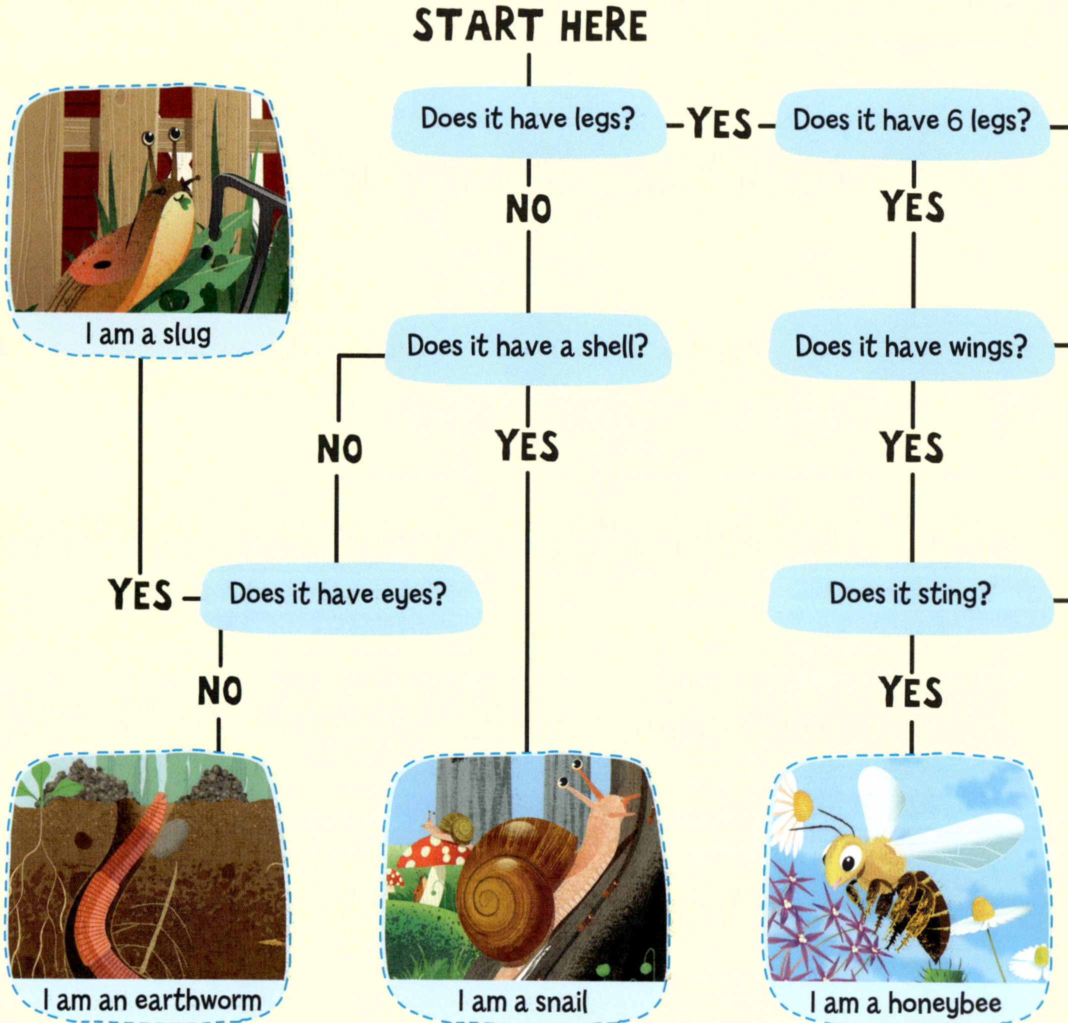

BUG HUNT

Go on a bug hunt around an outside space near you and see what bugs you can find. Make your own chart or take this one with you so you can identify them as you go along. Make sure to leave the bugs in their hiding places after you've finished identifying them!

NO
I am a millipede
NO
Does it make a web?
YES
NO
I am a caterpillar
I am a spider
NO
Is it active at night?
NO
YES
I am a firefly
I am a butterfly
WHAT BUGS ARE WE?

GLOSSARY

Burrow (verb) – to make a hole or tunnel, usually to live in.

Chrysalis – a hard case that protects a caterpillar while it changes into a moth or butterfly.

Fungi – a group of living things, including mushrooms, truffles, and yeasts, that are neither plants nor animals.

Microbes – very small living things that can only be seen using a microscope.

Nectar – a sweet liquid that flowers make. Bees, butterflies, and some other insects eat it.

Nocturnal – creatures that sleep in the day and come out at night.

Pests – annoying or troublesome things. For example, bugs that eat people's plants and food are considered pests.

Pollen – a dusty powder made by some flowers. Plants need pollen from flowers to make seeds.

Predators – animals that hunt and kill other animals for food.

Prolegs – small, fleshy body parts that look and act like legs but aren't actually legs.

Sap – a watery substance that comes out of a plant or tree.

Segments – pieces of something that can be separated.